罗莎·帕克斯

Heroes and Role Models | Non-Fiction Series

Copyright © 2022 by Level Learning, INC. and Washington Yu Ying PCS™
Original and Edited Text Copyright © 2022 by Washington Yu Ying PCS™

All rights reserved. No part of this book in whole or part may be reproduced without written permission from the publisher.

Published by Level Learning, INC.

Content Contributors:
Washington Yu Ying PCS™
Level Learning - Jingyao Qi

Illustrations by: Matt Austin

Leveling classification based on Level Learning standard.
For full description, visit www.levellearning.com

ISBN 978-1-64040-007-8
Simplified Chinese Edition

About Level Learning:

Level Learning provides a literacy focused curriculum specifically designed for K-12 Chinese as a Second Language classrooms. Our program offers 20 levels of specific and detailed objectives, leveled texts and passages, mastery-based online assessment, and analytics to enable data-driven instruction. Level Learning reading curriculum for both literature and informational text emphasize grammar and comprehension skills to help teachers develop confident and independent Chinese language readers. The non-fiction series of books are specifically designed to support our informational text course based on multiple national standards. To learn more about our entire offering, visit www.levellearning.com.

About Washington Yu Ying PCS™:

Washington Yu Ying PCS is a Mandarin English dual language immersion International Baccalaureate (IB) World school. Yu Ying's mission is to inspire and prepare young people to create a better world by challenging them to reach their full potential in a nurturing Chinese/English educational environment. Yu Ying's comprehensive IB, dual immersion curriculum equips students with global competencies for success in the real world. As a leader in immersion education, Yu Ying is determined to advance Chinese language programs and global citizenry education by helping other schools create and strengthen their Chinese programs. For more information, email: products@washingtonyuying.org

罗莎·帕克斯是一位非洲裔美国人。她出生于1913年2月4日。

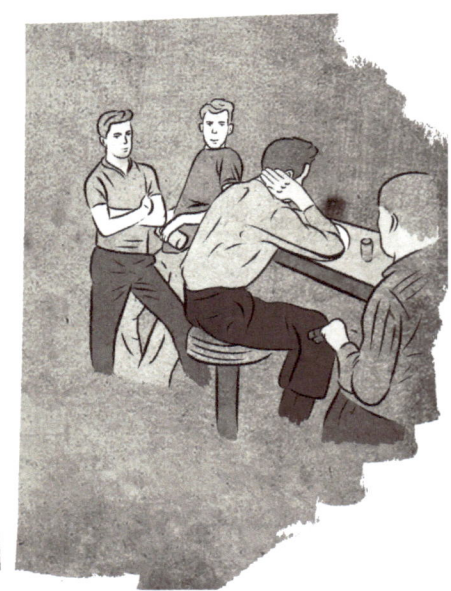

那时的美国很不平等。白人上白人的学校,非洲裔上非洲裔的学校。非洲裔不可以去白人的餐厅吃饭。

白人可以坐在巴士的前面，可是非洲裔要坐在巴士的后面。

罗莎·帕克斯觉得这样不对。她觉得白人和非洲裔应该是平等的。

她在巴士上坐在白人的座位上。因为这件事,她被关了起来。

她很**勇敢**地说出这些不平等。因为她的努力,白人和非洲裔在巴士上可以坐在一起了。

罗莎·帕克斯改变了美国的历史。她促进了美国白人与非洲裔的平等，让美国变得更公平。

Glossary

	Pinyin	English Definition
非洲裔	fēi zhōu yì	African descent
平等	píng děng	equalilty
餐厅	cān tīng	restaurant
巴士	bā shì	bus
觉得	jué de	to feel
关	guān	lock up
勇敢	yǒng gǎn	brave
改变	gǎi biàn	to change
历史	lì shǐ	history
促进	cù jìn	to promote

www.ingramcontent.com/pod-product-compliance
Lightning Source LLC
Chambersburg PA
CBHW041226070526
44584CB00001B/112